DATE DUE

HIGHSMITH #45115

THIS IS THE
PROMISE

By NORMAN BEASLEY

THE CROSS AND THE CROWN
The History of Christian Science

THE CONTINUING SPIRIT
The Story of Christian Science Since 1910

THIS IS THE PROMISE

THIS IS THE
PROMISE

NORMAN BEASLEY

DUELL, SLOAN AND PEARCE

New York

MANUFACTURED IN THE UNITED STATES OF AMERICA

VAN REES PRESS • NEW YORK

To
my mother, Letitia
and
my wife, Wilma

Contents

THIS IS THE
PROMISE

The Bible

ITS ARK of bullrushes and its manger have purified the
hearts of Jew and Gentile.

Its Ten Commandments, its crossing of the Red Sea,
its Sermon on the Mount, and its walk to Emmaus are
coins of brighter gold than can be found in all the world.

In its Testaments are wisdom and instruction, all in
affirmation of the infinitude of God.

This is the Bible.

Those who search this book know, as wrote Isaiah:

"For as the rain cometh down, and the snow from
heaven, and returneth not thither, but watereth the earth,

and maketh it bring forth and bud, that it may give seed to the sower, and bread to the eater:

"So shall my word be that goeth forth out of my mouth: it shall not return unto me void, but it shall accomplish that which I please, and it shall prosper *in the thing* whereto I sent it.

"For ye shall go out with joy, and be led forth with peace...."

Those who know this book understand, as wrote John:

"Behold, what manner of love the Father hath bestowed upon us, that we should be called the sons of God: therefore the world knoweth us not, because it knew him not.

"Beloved, now are we the sons of God, and it doth not yet appear what we shall be: but we know that, when he shall appear, we shall be like him; for we shall see him as he is.

"And every man that hath this hope in him purifieth himself, even as he is pure."

∽∽∾

Inexhaustible in wisdom, and patient in instruction, the Bible is an open door for all who would enter into the kingdom.

In the depth of his sorrow over war, Lincoln wrote to a friend, "I am profitably engaged in reading the Bible."

The dying Sir Walter Scott asked a companion, "Read to me from the book."

"What book?"

"Need you ask?" questioned Scott. "There is but one."

The Night Was History

To Bethlehem from Galilee came Joseph and his wife, Mary, to pay the taxes Caesar Augustus had decreed the world should pay. *There was no room for them in the inn,* and Mary, who was great with child, found a resting place in a stable behind the inn.

Here, a few nights later, the stars shone with a special brightness; and the night was history.

Not history in the sense of decree and punishment, but history that brought the guarantee that war, poverty, pestilence, sickness, and death, everything that is evil—everything!—is marked for eviction from the affairs of men.

Mankind does not yet accept this great truth, but acceptance will come. The triumph of the brightness of Christmas over the darkness of evil is inevitable.

Once in history, the day was only a moment; now, without the moment, all history is without understanding.

At the Same Price

THE TEMPTER came when Jesus was hungry, and said: "If thou be the Son of God, command that these stones be made bread."

But Jesus answered, saying: "It is written, Man shall not live by bread alone, but by every word that proceedeth out of the mouth of God."

The tempter tried a second time. Leading Jesus to the pinnacle of the temple, he said, tauntingly:

"If thou be the Son of God, cast thyself down: for it is written, He shall give his angels charge concerning thee:

and in *their* hands they shall bear thee up, lest at any time thou cast thy foot against a stone."

Failing again, the tempter took Jesus up into the high mountain, "and sheweth him all the kingdoms of the world, and the glory of them;

"And saith unto him, All these things will I give thee, if thou wilt fall down and worship me."

What the tempter was seeking to do was to insinuate doubt into the mind of Jesus that He was, as the voice at the river said He was, "my beloved Son, in which I am well pleased."

Doubt never came.

Whether in the temple, in the synagogue, or by the sea, Jesus spoke of God as the Father, of Himself as the Son, and of all men as children of God, even according to the gospel of St. John:

"He came unto his own, and his own received him not.

"But as many as received him, to them gave he power to become the Sons of God."

In its preoccupation with the things of the flesh, mankind is disposed to accept the low estimate the tempter has placed upon it. It is a preoccupation of which Paul spoke in addressing the Romans:

"For they that are after the flesh do mind the things of the flesh; but they that are after the Spirit, the things of the Spirit. . . .

"The Spirit itself beareth witness with our spirit, that we are the children of God:

"And if children, then heirs; heirs of God, and joint heirs with Christ; if so be that we suffer with *him,* that we may be also glorified together.

"For I reckon that the sufferings of this present time *are* not worthy *to be compared* with the glory which shall be revealed in us."

From the vantage point of accepting Sonship with God, Jesus saw He could have the material possessions the tempter offered; or He could have what is given of God— *at the same price.*

He need worship only One, or the other.

In Full Measure

He had not yet chosen His disciples and this day, as Jesus stood on the shore of the Lake of Gennesareth, "the people pressed against him to hear the word of God."

Looking about, He saw two fishing boats close by, and calling to Simon, the owner of one, He asked the fisherman to "thrust out a little from the land. And he sat down, and taught the people out of the ship."

As on the other side of Galilee, where a hillside was a sufficient pulpit, so here in Capernaum was a fisherman's boat a house of prayer. On the hillside, or by the sea, in the synagogue, in the temple, by the well of Jacob, or in the house of the chief of the Pharisees, the words He spoke were in full measure:

"My sheep hear my voice, and I know them, and they follow me: and I give them eternal life: and they shall never perish, neither shall any *man* pluck them out of my hand."

Words such as these need no altar, for they are life; need no sanctuary, for they are love; and need no witness, for they are truth.

The Sermon on the Mount

THE MULTITUDES were gathered on the hillside, coming from Galilee, and *from* Decapolis, and *from* Jerusalem, and *from* Judea, and *from* beyond Jordan; and He was saying:

"Blessed *are* the poor in spirit: for theirs is the kingdom of heaven. Blessed *are* they that mourn: for they shall be comforted. Blessed *are* the meek: for they shall inherit the earth. Blessed *are* they which do hunger and thirst after righteousness: for they shall be filled. Blessed *are* the merciful: for they shall obtain mercy. Blessed *are* the pure in heart: for they shall see God."

He was speaking not as men speak within the walls of a temple, but as a man speaks in the open fields with the grasses and flowers at his feet; or, under the wide cedars, with the birds singing above his words; or, on the mountains, with the white clouds for companions, and the west wind in his face.

Where than under the open sky should first have been heard the words:

"Our Father which art in heaven, Hallowed be thy name. Thy kingdom come. Thy will be done on earth, as *it is* in heaven. Give us this day our daily bread. And forgive us our debts, as we forgive our debtors. And lead us not into temptation, but deliver us from evil: For thine is the kingdom, and the power, and the glory, for ever. Amen."

Where than among the hills and valleys, with the sun shining upon Him, should He have said:

"Therefore all things whatsoever ye would that men should do to you, do ye even so to them."

Not all in the multitudes that listened understood His words. Only a few understood. On that day, even as now, the people were astonished at His doctrine.

"Is Not This the Carpenter?"

JESUS WAS in His own country again, and among His own people. They were a mixed people. There were Jews; also, there were Syrians, Arabs, a few Greeks, Phoenicians—and they mingled together so freely, and so well, that Galilee was known as the "Circle of the Gentiles."

As a child, Jesus played in the stony paths and narrow streets of Nazareth; as a youth, and as a young man, He knew the mountains that shut off the great plains of Esdraelon.

From the summit above the village, He could see the outlines of Carmel, where Elijah flung his challenge to the priests of Baal; the city of Shechem, where Rehoboam, the son of Solomon, found only bitterness because of heavy taxes; the hills of Gilboa, where Saul and three of his sons were felled in battle with the Philistines; the two peaks above Megiddo, where the voice of Zephaniah, the prophet, was heard over the voice of Josiah, the king. . . .

And on the far horizon, between the mountains of Shunem and Tabor, was the valley of the Jordan and the river over which Moses led the tribes of Israel into the land of Canaan.

Steadily, in summer and in winter, the winds swept over the holy places and across Nazareth, stirring its vines and fig trees in summer, and sharply closing its doors in winter.

Doubtless, His home was much like the others in the village, and the countryside—a hut of stone that served as shop and kitchen by day and bedroom at night; and having for furnishings, a few cushions on the ground, a mat, a clay pot, or two, perhaps a painted chest; and, of course, the tools to work with.

Here in Nazareth, Joseph had his shop in which Jesus learned to be a carpenter; here, His sisters were married; His brothers grew to manhood; here, too, Mary must have thought, often, of the moment of prophecy before she was wed to Joseph.

And now, He was preaching in the synagogue, having come back to His own people from the country of the Gadarenes where He had healed the man possessed with the devil, the woman with the plague, and had raised from the dead the daughter of Jairus.

Astonished at His words, and wondering about His fame, many whispered among themselves: "From whence hath this *man* these things? and what wisdom *is* this which is given unto him, that even such mighty works are wrought by his hand?

"Is not this carpenter, the son of Mary, the brother of James, and Joses, and of Juda, and Simon? and are not his sisters here with us?"

They remembered Him as a boy going to the village school; they knew Him to be untutored in the ancient traditions of the Law; they thought of Him as a carpenter and they were afraid; as in the country of the Gadarenes, when He had healed the man possessed of the devil, the multitude had asked that He depart from their midst.

Because they were afraid and, too, because Galilaeans had come to think of themselves as an inferior people (as was said of them in Jerusalem), they did not believe His words, nor accept His works—and so great was the hostility that surrounded Him that "he could there do no mighty work, save that he laid his hands upon a few sick folk, and healed *them*. And he marvelled because of their unbelief."

Now about thirty years old, and in the first steps of His ministry, Jesus did not comprehend hostility and disbelief.

He had yet to say:

"The words that I speak unto you I speak not of myself: but the Father that dwelleth within me, he doeth the works"; yet to confirm Peter's recognition: "Thou art the Christ, the Son of the living God."

Deep, deep within Him had come the understanding that, having been created by God "in his *own* image," His was the will of God, the words of God, and the acts of God. Believing thus, He knew no obstacles; and, in testimony of the eternal nature of *all* men, offered His work in the sepulchre.

He was a carpenter. The walls He built are held together by His truth and love; the doors He made are not shut to the streets; the windows He shaped are open to the sky.

The Great Temple

OFTEN, with His disciples, Jesus came to the Mount of Olives, to sit on its slope and look out across Jerusalem.

At His feet was the great temple with its sunlit terraces, its porticoes which were eight years in building, its shining roof, its wide terraces—and over the voices of devotion was the smell of cattle and sheep and dung, the blood of slaughtered animals, the cries of venders pressing their wares, and the noise of counting at the tables of the money-changers.

It was in the temple that Jesus, when in Jerusalem, spent

much of His time. In it, and in Jerusalem, He heard little, and saw little, that pleased Him.

There was the boastful display of pretended learning by the Pharisees, and their eager desire to debate the trivialities of the Law; there was the disrespect of the priests for the holy things of the temple; there was the desecration of the sanctuary, which had been made into a market place.

In this city, and in this temple, the priests were suppliants to materiality; and, defiled by intrigue, the high priests were suppliants to politics. Higher than the high priests was the sovereign pontiff, whose office was so profitable that its occupant was a Roman official who was frequently replaced that another favorite might be rewarded. Overlooking the temple was the tower of Antonia, a headquarters for Roman troops, and from whose walls soldiers could watch the activities in the enclosure below, and observe the gates to the temple.

The gates were guarded by the chosen of the high priests, and their duty was to make sure that none crossed to the inner gate who was carrying a stick, or a parcel, who had dusty shoes, or who took a short cut; and, also, that none entered the inner gate unless in a state of cleanliness, according to the Law.

Daily, the people came to this center of a nation's activities to listen to canonical instruction, to hear religious discussions, to settle legal disputes; and to worship and to trade, one with another.

A Galilaean, Jesus was ridiculed and insulted, as were all Galilaeans, even though they came not as merchants, but as pilgrims. Contemptuously, it was asked of them as Nathanael asked of Jesus, "Can any good thing come out of Nazareth?"

Every day, when he was in Jerusalem, He preached in the temple. There were few who believed. Of course, the man who was born blind, the man who had dropsy, the woman who was bent with infirmity, and the woman who was taken in adultery, they believed, as did the many others who were healed. His words and His works were whips that scourged priest and Pharisee, alike.

And so they put Him to death; and every throne, every empire, and every reigning philosophy that existed then has vanished—as they must always vanish before the most martial force there is, truth and love.

The Villages by the Sea

THIS WAS the place toward which His steps often turned when He was weary of disbelief. This was Capernaum, by the Sea of Galilee. It was in Galilee He chose all but one of His disciples. The one was Judas Iscariot. It was in Capernaum, in the home of Peter, He always found shelter.

Now Jesus was in Capernaum again, having come from Nazareth where, only hours before, the people rose up in their disbelief "and thrust him out of the city, and led him unto the brow of the hill whereon their city was built, that they might cast him down headlong."

In a synagogue, on this Sabbath Day in Capernaum, He healed "a man which had a spirit of an unclean devil." He healed Peter's mother-in-law of a great fever; and, when the sun was setting and the sick and afflicted were gathered about the door to Peter's house, He went to them and healed them, all.

The next day, early in the morning, He departed Peter's house, and went into the desert. But the people followed Him, and remained near. It was always this way in the fishing village by the waters of Galilee. Here lived His true family.

A simple people, their minds were not darkened by titles and ritual. They heard His words, saw His works, understood with their hearts, and were healed.

There was beauty in a land that without Him would be without history.

Fourteen miles long, eight miles wide, one hundred and fifty feet deep at its deepest, the Sea of Galilee was nearly seven hundred feet below the level of the Mediterranean, some thirty miles to the west. Closed in by mountains on the south, and opening into the Plain of Gennesareth on the north and west, the sea came gently to the shore where, close by Capernaum, were Chorazin, Bethsaida, and Dalmanutha. The sea, the hillsides, and the villages formed the center of His ministry.

In this, His own country, He restored the daughter of Jairus; healed the woman who touched His clothes of a sickness that had plagued her twelve years; healed Mary, called Magdalene; came to His disciples walking upon the water. Here He found peace after the beheading of John the Baptist, fed the multitude, turned the water into wine, healed the son of a nobleman, and sat with His disciples after the Crucifixion.

Many times He must have lingered upon the rising hills, and looked upon the villages, with their dwellings and fountains, synagogues and temples; upon the valleys, rich with vegetation; toward the sea, the many boats, the fishermen, and their nets drying upon the shore; followed with His eyes the grebes and gulls and pelicans wheeling and diving into the clear waters.

To the east and to the north, where the Jordan joined the sea, was the hillside where gathered the multitudes from Galilee, and *from* Decapolis, and *from* Jerusalem, and *from* Judea, and *from* beyond Jordan to hear Him preach of worldly things and of God's kingdom.

It was a bright and fertile land. Almond blossoms nodded in the soft, warm air; olive trees wore their garments of green and silver; all the year the hills and valleys were hued with flowers and fruits and grains and vegetation, as nature brought the miracle of her abundance.

It was a lively and busy land. There were ships, and shipbuilders, and trade. Romans on military and civil duty were stationed there; mingling with the population of Jews and Gentiles and Arabs were merchants from the Nile, and from the Euphrates—altogether, more than two million people lived in the hills, in the valleys, and on the plains of Galilee.

⌁⌁⌁

Little remains of what was a prosperous society. No longer are the hills and valleys hued with flowers and fruits and grains and vegetation. No longer is the Sea of Galilee busy with the ships of fishermen. Nothing remains of Capernaum. Nothing remains of Chorazin, Bethsaida, and Dalmanutha, so that men are no longer sure where they were.

But the names of Capernaum, Chorazin, Bethsaida, and Dalmanutha will be remembered to the end of the world because, in them, a Man spoke with understanding.

Simon Called Peter

THEY ALL remembered the first time they saw Him.
Simon and his brother Andrew remembered. They
were casting a net in the Sea of Galilee when they saw
Him walking along the shore, and heard Him calling
upon them to follow Him. James and John, the sons of
Zebedee, remembered. They were mending their nets
when He called. Simon's mother-in-law remembered. She
was sick of a fever, and He healed her.

On that same day when He called Simon and Andrew,
James and John, and healed the mother-in-law of Simon,
others saw Him and remembered because, before the day

was ended, many who were sick had come to Him, and were healed.

Here on the shore of the Sea of Galilee, in the home of Simon, He found a retreat to which He returned, again and again, in the high years of His assignment. Here lived those who loved Him; and they listened wonderingly as He told them, "Is not the life more than meat, and the body than raiment"; as they watched with awe when "they brought to him a man sick of the palsy, lying on a bed," and heard Him say, "Arise, take up thy bed, and go unto thine house." And the man took up his bed, "and departed to his house."

In this community, called Capernaum, the young Master found peaceful neighbors and, in Simon, called Peter, a forthright disciple.

Fishing was the principal work of the people; and as Jesus, with His gentle compassion, had charm for them, so did Peter, with his stubborn integrity, have appeal for Jesus. Peter's home was His home; Peter's house was a meeting place for His followers; Peter's boat was a pulpit when the multitudes were on the shore.

One day, after preaching to a multitude, Jesus said to Peter: "Launch out into the deep, and let down your nets."

With Andrew, Peter had fished all the night before without gain. This time so many fish were caught that the net broke. James and John came to help, but the fish were so many that "they filled the ships, so they began to sink."

Frightened, Peter pleaded, "Depart from me; for I am a sinful man, O Lord."

Charging Peter to "fear not," Jesus promised to make him a fisher of men. And so Peter became, from that day.

Impetuous and without guile, Peter was not without doubt.

There was the night of the storm when Jesus came walking on the water. Peter stepped out of the boat to go to Him. Losing courage, he began to sink, but stretching forth His hand, Jesus "caught him, and said unto him, O thou of little faith, wherefore didst thou doubt?"

Yet, with his doubt, it was Peter who was nearest Him. After Peter were James and John. These three were with Jesus when He raised the daughter of Jairus; they were with Him at the Transfiguration; they went with Him to watch while He prayed in Gethsemane.

But, wherever they went, it was Peter who was looked upon as leader among the disciples. It was he who paid the taxes; and, after many disciples "walked no more with him," and Jesus inquired of the twelve who remained, "Will ye also go away?" it was Peter who answered for the rest:

"Lord, to whom shall we go; thou hast the words of eternal life."

It was Peter who was first to perceive that Jesus was the Messiah.

"When Jesus came into the coasts of Caesarea Philippi, he asked his disciples, saying, Whom do men say that I the Son of God am? And they said, Some *say that thou art* John the Baptist; some, Elias; and others, Jeremias, or one of the prophets. He said unto them, But whom say ye that I am?

"And Simon Peter answered and said, Thou art the Christ, the Son of the living God."

❦❦❦

Thou art the Christ, the Son of the living God.

This was recognition that brought immediate reply:

"And Jesus answered and said unto him, Blessed art thou, Simon Bar-jona: for flesh and blood hath not revealed *it* unto thee, but my Father which is in heaven. And I say unto thee, That thou art Peter, and upon this rock I will build my church; and the gates of hell shall not prevail against it."

Upon this rock I will build my church.

It was a church He intended should be governed by

spirit and by truth—and not by the doctrines of men. It was a church He intended should remain forever His—and that Peter might be forever honored among men, Jesus chose to honor him before God.

He Wrote on the Ground

THE WOMAN was charged with adultery, and, after saying, "Moses in the law commanded us, that such should be stoned," the scribes and Pharisees asked Him:

"What sayest thou?"

Instead of answering, Jesus leaned over and wrote on the ground with His finger.

The woman's accusers continued to ask until, looking up, Jesus said: "He that is without sin among you, let him first cast a stone at her"; and once more wrote on the ground.

When He looked up again only the woman was before

Him. Tormented by their own guilt, the scribes and Pharisees had gone out "one by one, beginning at the eldest, *even* unto the last."

Seeing this, Jesus asked: "Where are those thine accusers? hath no man condemned thee?"

She answered, "No man"; and He said to her, "Neither do I condemn thee: go, and sin no more."

Neither do I condemn thee. To those who judged after the flesh, these were extraordinary words. They seemed to overlook wrong; but they did not. They seemed to join the guilt of the woman with the guilt of the scribes and Pharisees, and condone both; but they did not.

He did not judge after the flesh; and because He did not, He could not condemn.

But He did say, "Go, and sin no more."

These were words of instruction. In them was the teaching that as the remembrance of having sinned is the punishment, so is continuance in sin the condemnation.

The Leaven of the Pharisees

H<small>E HEALED</small> the sick, fed the multitudes, and restored
the dead, and still the Pharisees questioned Him,
seeking a sign from heaven.

Aware of their deceit, Jesus rebuked them, saying, "Why
doth this generation seek after a sign? verily, I say unto
you, There shall no sign be given unto this generation."

Departing, Jesus entered into the ship and left Dalmanutha for the other shore. As they traveled the waters of
Galilee, He learned that the disciples had forgotten to
bring bread. "And he charged them, saying, Take heed,

beware of the leaven of the Pharisees, and *of* the leaven of Herod."

Not comprehending His words, the disciples reasoned that He was displeased because of what they had forgotten. It was not that, for He said to them:

"Why reason ye, because ye have no bread? perceive ye not yet, neither understand? have ye your heart yet hardened?"

Have ye your heart yet hardened? That was His question—not, "has your heart been hardened?" but, *have ye your heart yet hardened?* Their lack of understanding troubled Him, for He continued to search the hidden places within them:

"Having eyes, see ye not? and having ears, hear ye not? and do ye not remember? When I brake the five loaves among five thousand, how many baskets full of fragments took ye up?"

They answered: "Twelve."

"And when the seven among four thousand, how many baskets full of fragments took ye up?"

They answered: "Seven."

And He said to them: "How is it that ye do not understand?"

And so, the two questions meet:

*How is it that ye do not understand? Have ye your heart
yet hardened?*

The time came when He spoke again to the disciples as
He had spoken while they traveled the waters of Galilee.
He was preaching to them, was urging them to avoid de-
ceiving themselves, and was saying: "Beware ye of the
leaven of the Pharisees, which is hypocrisy"; and what,
hitherto, they failed to comprehend, they now began to
understand.

All but one.

It was not until after Pilate had washed his hands that
Iscariot began to understand what he had eaten when he
partook of the leaven of the Pharisees.

The Servant of All

THE TWELVE DISCIPLES were with Jesus on the way to Capernaum and they fell to arguing as to which among them was the greatest; and when they were in Capernaum, and in Peter's house, He asked:

"What was it that ye disputed among yourselves by the way?"

None among them offered an answer, but knowing their thoughts, He said to them: "If any man desire to be first, *the same* shall be last of all, and servant of all.

"And he took a child, and set him in the midst of them"; and said to them: "Whosoever shall receive one of such children in my name, receiveth me: and whosoever shall receive me, receiveth not me, but him that sent me."

There was another day in Judea when the disciples rebuked those who "brought young children to him, that he should touch them"; and "when Jesus saw *it,* he was much displeased, and said unto them, Suffer little children to come unto me, and forbid them not: for of such is the kingdom of God."

Walking with Jesus on the way to Jerusalem, James and John listened while their mother requested that "these my two sons may sit, the one on thy right hand, and the other on the left, in thy kingdom."

To the mother, and to her sons, He said: "To sit on my right hand, and on my left, is not mine to give, but *it shall be given to them* for whom it is prepared of my Father."

Together, on another occasion, the disciples asked, "Who is the greatest in the kingdom of heaven?" and taking a little child in His arms, Jesus answered:

"Verily I say unto you, Except ye be converted, and become as little children, ye shall not enter into the kingdom of heaven.

"Whosoever therefore shall humble himself as this little child, the same is greatest in the kingdom of heaven."

There were many times when the disciples argued as to which among them was the greatest. Knowing of their disagreement, Jesus neglected no opportunity to impress upon them that possession of the Kingdom is found only in the divine innocence of a little child.

In their search for greatness, the disciples saw only the vestments. Jesus saw only the soul.

Thomas

H IS NAME was Thomas, which is called Didymus; and for his doubt he is remembered.

The Crucifixion was over, and eight days had gone since Jesus had appeared to the disciples; and Thomas, who had not been present, would not believe when they told him, and scoffed, saying: "Except I shall see in his hands the print of the nails, and put my finger into the print of the nails, and thrust my hand into his side, I will not believe."

Again the disciples were gathered in a room in Jerusalem when Jesus once more appeared in their midst; and this time, Thomas, who was present, heard Him say:

"Reach hither thy finger, and behold my hands; and reach hither thy hand, and thrust *it* into my side: and be not faithless, but believing."

Thomas disbelieved no longer.

Jesus was persistent. Placing His heel on what had been the disciple's unbelief, He said: "Thomas, because thou hast seen me, thou hast believed: blessed *are* they that have not seen, and *yet* have believed."

In Jordan where Jesus had gone to escape death by stoning, word came to Him that, in Bethany, Lazarus was sick. After two days, Jesus said to His disciples: "Let us go into Judaea again."

The protest was quick. "Master," they cried, "the Jews of late sought to stone thee: and goest thou thither again?"

He talked with them, and still they protested, until He told them: "Lazarus is dead," and added, "Let us go unto him."

In their fear, the disciples were silent. All but one. Thomas, which is called Didymus, said to them, "Let us also go, that we may die with him"; and so saying, fell in step with the firstborn of Mary.

"Will Ye Also Go Away?"

THERE HAD BEEN five barley loaves and two small fishes to feed the multitude; and now, as the disciples gathered up the fragments, and filled twelve baskets, the people pressed forward to take Jesus by force, and make Him a king. Perceiving their intentions, He departed quickly, and alone.

Unabashed, they followed Him, and found Him in Capernaum, and inquired: "Rabbi, when camest thou hither?"

Understanding why they came, Jesus said:

"Verily, verily, I say unto you, Ye seek me not because ye saw the miracles, but because ye did eat of the loaves, and were filled."

Whereupon, He taught them, saying: "Labour not for the meat which perisheth, but for that meat which endureth unto everlasting life"; and went on: "Verily, verily, I say unto you, Except ye eat the flesh of the Son of man, and drink his blood, ye have no life in you."

Having so said, He emphasized:

"Whoso eateth my flesh, and drinketh my blood, hath eternal life: and I will raise him up at the last day. For my flesh is meat indeed, and my blood is drink indeed. He that eateth my flesh, and drinketh my blood, dwelleth in me, and I in him. As the living Father hath sent me, and I live by the Father: so he that eateth me, even he shall live by me."

These were words too hard for the ears of most who heard them, for they asked: "Is not this Jesus, the son of Joseph, whose father and mother we know?" and asked again: "How can this man give us *his* flesh to eat?"

They did not understand that he was speaking not of himself as the son of Joseph, and not of himself as the flesh and blood of Mary, but of Himself and the truth into which He was born as the Son of God; was saying that truth alone can impart truth; and was calling upon all who heard Him to believe, as later He called upon His disciples to believe, that "when he, the Spirit of truth, is come, he will guide you into all truth."

ᏋᏋᏋ

A restiveness was upon the people and they murmured among themselves, causing Jesus to ask, "Doth this offend you?" and then to reaffirm His testimony:

"It is the spirit that quickeneth; the flesh profiteth nothing: the words that I speak unto you, *they* are spirit, and *they* are life."

Angered that He should continue to speak in a manner that displeased them, many who had walked with Him turned away, and saw Him no more. Watching them go, Jesus said unto the twelve who remained: "Will ye also go away?

"Then Simon Peter answered him, Lord, to whom shall we go? thou hast the words of eternal life."

Peter spoke amiss. Of the twelve, there was one who did go away so that, of the hundreds He sent out to bear witness of Him, and of the multitudes that saw His works, only eleven remained who believed He came to offer the works of God, and not to enshrine the flesh of men.

The multitudes would have made Jesus a king; He chose to wash the feet of those who remained His disciples.

"Soever Ye Desire"

JESUS OFTEN talked about prayer, often spoke of faith. On a slope by the Sea of Galilee, He instructed the multitudes in how to pray, saying, "When thou prayest, enter into thy closet, and when thou hast shut thy door, pray to thy Father which is in secret; and thy Father which seeth in secret shall reward thee openly.

"But when ye pray, use not vain repetitions, as the heathen *do*: for they think that they shall be heard for their much speaking.

"Be not ye therefore like unto them: for your Father knoweth what things ye have need of, before ye ask him," whereupon He gave the multitudes the manner in which they should pray.

With His disciples, He had spent the night in Bethany and, in the morning, on the way to Jerusalem, He talked with the twelve who walked with Him:

"For verily I say unto you, That whosoever shall say unto this mountain, Be thou removed, and be thou cast into the sea; and shall not doubt in his heart, but shall believe that those things which he saith shall come to pass; he shall have whatsoever he saith.

"Therefore, I say unto you, What things soever ye desire, when ye pray, believe that ye receive *them,* and ye shall have *them.*"

And cautioned:

"And when ye stand praying, forgive, if ye have ought against any: that your Father also which is in heaven may forgive your trespasses.

"But if ye do not forgive, neither will your Father which is in heaven forgive your trespasses."

❧❧❧

Jesus believed Himself to be the Son of God, and not the son of Joseph; and because He so believed, the doubts that beset mankind found in Him no footing. Having a faith that knew only truth, He rebuked the barren fig tree and caused it to dry "up from the roots," as He rebuked the wind and the sea, and caused them to be still.

His disciples did not know, as did He, that whether wind or water, mountain or tree, nature is subject to the one Will that alone rules the universe; and that it must obey all who believe and who pray—because *only* when man believes, and prays, is he worthy to receive what is asked.

Wherever the People

THERE WAS division among the people concerning the Nazarene, but not among the chief priests and Pharisees. Only a few days before, the Pharisees had sent the officers to seize Him that His words might not be heard by the people; but the officers returned without Him.

"Why have ye not brought him?" the officers were asked, and they answered: "Never man spake like this man."

Angered, the Pharisees said: "Are ye also deceived? Have any of the rulers or of the Pharisees believed on him? But this people who knoweth not the law are cursed."

Often, the chief priests and Pharisees spoke among themselves of ways to keep His words from reaching the ears of the people, and thereby curse them before the Law.

And now He was in the temple again, teaching. It was early in the morning, and seeing the people gathered about Him, the Pharisees edged their way near to where he sat, to ask questions, and to dispute His words, that they might find occasion to kill Him.

They questioned Him about the Law, rejected His answers, denied His testimony of Himself, and heard Him say, "The Father that sent me beareth witness unto me." They asked many questions, and they did not understand His words although, among the people, were those who did understand; and to those who did understand, He said:

"If ye continue in my word, *then* are ye my disciples indeed"; and promised: "And ye shall know the truth, and the truth shall make you free."

⟡⟡⟡

The time came when the chief priests and the Pharisees did kill Him; but to this day, whatever the land, and wherever the people, the land is free, and the people are free only as they have continued in the Word—not in the word of man, but *in* the word of God.

The Great Commandment

IN BETHANY Lazarus had come forth *"from the place* where the dead was laid,"* and the chief priests and Pharisees took counsel together.

They were afraid; and there was cause. Here was a Prophet who spoke of God as dwelling in the hearts of men, and not in the subtleties of the Law, nor in the traditions of the altar; a Prophet who spoke of mercy and not of vengeance, of forgiveness and not of hate; a Teacher who said love of God was *all* the Law.

Seeing men and women as children of God, Jesus called upon them to worship, not as Jews, nor as Gentiles, Romans, Greeks, or Syrians, but as children of God; and required of them that they worship in spirit and in truth.

They were teachings that distinguished between what was spiritual and what was material, separated the eternal from the temporal, and left no room for intermediaries between God and man. Whether priest or publican, it was a religion in which all men were equal.

A wholly revolutionary religion, it provoked the chief priests and Pharisees to say among themselves, "If we let him thus alone, all *men* will believe on him: and the Romans shall come and take away both our place and nation"; and Caiaphas, the high priest, to decide, "It is expedient for us, that one man should die for the people, and that the whole nation perish not."

The chief priests and the Pharisees had much trouble with this Man from Galilee.

There was the time when they censured Him, inquiring: "Why walk not thy disciples according to the tradition of the elders, but eat bread with unwashen hands?"

Answering, He said:

"Well hath Esaias prophesied of you hypocrites, as it is written, This people honoureth me with *their* lips, but their heart is far from me. Howbeit in vain do they worship me, teaching *for* doctrines the commandments of men. For laying aside the commandment of God, ye hold the tradition of men, *as* the washing of pots and cups: and many other such like things ye do"; and added:

"Full well ye reject the commandment of God, that ye may keep your own tradition."

There was another time when, among the Pharisees, was one who was a lawyer, and he asked a tempting question:

"Master, which *is* the great commandment in the law?"

And Jesus replied:

"Thou shalt love the Lord thy God with all thy heart, and with all thy soul, and with all thy mind. This is the first and great commandment. And the second *is* like unto it, Thou shalt love thy neighbour as thyself.

"On these two commandments hang all the law and the prophets."

In the upstairs room on the night of Gethsemane, He again instructed His disciples on how to be true citizens of the Kingdom of God:

"A new commandment I give unto you, That ye love one another; as I have loved you, that ye also love one another.

"By this shall all *men* know that ye are my disciples, if ye have love one to another."

The hate that cried, "Crucify him," was destroyed in the love of which He spoke. It is love that is of God, and knows only God. It is love that may be trusted, forever.

"How Long Halt Ye?"

TOLD IT was Jesus of Nazareth who was passing, the blind man set up such an outcry that Jesus sent for him, and asked:

"What wilt thou that I should do unto thee?"

And the blind man answered: "Lord, that I might receive my sight.

"And Jesus said unto him, Go thy way: thy faith hath made thee whole."

Thy faith hath made thee whole. These were repeated

words in His ministry. They were heard by the woman who "had suffered many things of many physicians," and who "had an issue of blood twelve years"; they were heard by the leper, who was one of ten who were cleansed.

There was Mary Magdalene to whom He said, "Thy faith hath saved thee; go in peace"; there was the faith of the centurion who asked that his servant be healed; there was the faith of the nobleman who "saith unto him, Sir, come down ere my child die."

Jesus never stood idle in the presence of sickness, nor could He understand unbelief that denied to God the power to "heal the sick, cleanse the lepers, raise the dead, cast out devils."

A thousand years before, Elijah saw the heritage of the children of Israel stained by unbelief, and he rebuked his people:

"How long halt ye between two opinions? If the Lord be God, follow him: if Baal, follow him."

To the multitudes on the hillside, Jesus said: "No man can serve two masters: for either he will hate the one, and love the other; or else he will hold to the one, and despise the other. Ye cannot serve God and mammon."

Jesus had no time to halt between two opinions.

Knowing he was one in spirit with God, even as a drop

of water is one in flood with the sea, He perceived, as he said to the scribes, "The Lord our God is one Lord."

He served no other. Seeing God as Spirit, worshiping in spirit and in truth, knowing that faith is one with prayer, and accepting only that which is eternal, He had authority over all that is temporal.

"Before Abraham Was"

O N THIS day in Jerusalem, Jesus was in the temple and the Pharisees were scornful of His words, for again He was talking of life; and He was saying:

"Verily, verily, I say unto you, If a man keep my saying, he shall never see death."

"Now we know that thou hast a devil," chorused the Pharisees. "Abraham is dead, and the prophets; and thou sayest, If a man keep my saying, he shall never taste of death."

"Your father Abraham rejoiced to see my day," answered Jesus, "and he saw *it,* and was glad."

Disbelieving, they challenged: "Thou art not yet fifty years old, and hast thou seen Abraham?"

And Jesus replied: "Verily, verily, I say unto you, Before Abraham was, I am."

On the night He went with His disciples to the garden, He spoke again of life, in this wise:

"And now, O Father, glorify thou me with thine own self with the glory which I had with thee before the world was."

On this night, as on the day in the temple, He was speaking not of breath, and not of form, and not of flesh, but of truth—and of truth as life, and of life as the eternal gift. On that day in the temple, as on this night with the disciples, He sought to use the cords of His illumined mind to draw the minds of all men into the Source of all life.

He knew, as He said when there "came to *him* certain of the Sadducees, which deny there is any resurrection," that "the dead are raised, even Moses shewed at the bush, when he calleth the Lord the God of Abraham, and the God of Isaac, and the God of Jacob.

"For he is not a God of the dead, but of the living: for all live unto him."

Farewell to Galilee

K NOWING THE portion that awaited Him in Jerusalem,
Jesus had absented Himself from the temple for
many months, perhaps eighteen in all, and had walked in
Galilee. Now, the feast of the tabernacles was near, and a
caravan was making ready for the pilgrimage to Jerusalem.

With his own family were brethren who viewed Him
with disfavor, and who wished that His enemies might do
away with Him, for they urged Him to go to Jerusalem
and "do the works that thou doest."

Undeceived, Jesus gave no heed to their words, and remained in Galilee, so that when the caravan came to Jeru-

salem His enemies sought Him at the feast, and finding Him not, inquired, "Where is he?"

They did not know, nor did his brethren, that already Jesus was nearing Jerusalem, having left Galilee in secret, with a few companions, after the departure of the caravan. It was in the autumn of the year that He took leave of the countryside He loved.

Gentle winds brushed leaves from His path; golden was the sky of late afternoon; along the way, flowers were wide to the sun, birds sang through the day and into the dusk; the fragrance of flowers and trees and the warm earth was in the haze that hung over the gathering hills. Everywhere, the miracle of the seed was declaring itself in the maturity of the vines and the olives, and the figs and palms.

Many times Jesus must have turned and looked back toward the Galilee of His boyhood, knowing He would not come again until He had fulfilled the mission for which He was sent. In the villages of Galilee, there were friends, and in the solitude of its hills, serenity—in contrast to Jerusalem, where none spoke openly for Him in fear of the ill will of the priesthood of the temple.

No Doubts to Feed

IN THE YEARS of His journey, Jesus visited many cities and many villages in Palestine, and He spoke of life many times, but never once did He speak of it in terms other than eternal.

In Jerusalem, from Solomon's porch at the feast of the dedication, He told His questioners: "My sheep hear my voice, and I know them, and they follow me: And I give unto them eternal life." In Samaria, near the well of Jacob, He said to His disciples: "Lift up your eyes, and look on the fields; for they are white already to harvest. And he that reapeth receiveth wages, and gathereth fruit into life eternal."

In Capernaum, in addressing the many, He referred to himself as "the bread which came down from heaven," and declared, "Verily, verily, I say unto you, He that believeth on me hath everlasting life."

It was evening, and He was instructing His disciples for the last time:

"Behold, the hour cometh, yea, is now come, that ye shall be scattered, every man to his own, and shall leave me alone: and yet I am not alone, because the Father is with me."

Then, lifting His words above the hour, Jesus spoke of God, of life, and of the work that was finished:

"And this is life eternal, that they might know thee the only true God, and Jesus Christ, whom thou hast sent.

"I have glorified thee on earth: I have finished the work which thou gavest me to do.

"And now, O Father, glorify thou me with thine own self with the glory which I had with thee before the world was."

Since the day He led His disciples as far as Bethany, and was parted from them, no one has accepted, as did He, the meaning of life. No one has known, as did He, that God is inseparable from His children; and *all* are His children. No one has understood, as did He, that all life is of God, and being of God life is eternal.

Jesus never believed the physical evidences of what men call death. He restored Lazarus, the daughter of Jairus, and the widow's son; and did so in obedience to "the Father which sent me.... I know that his commandment is life everlasting: whatsoever I speak therefore, even as the Father said unto me, so I speak."

Living only in God, Jesus knew life to be true to itself; and, being true to itself, to be undividable. Having found His real home with the Maker of only that which is eternal, He had no doubts to feed with the crumbs mankind calls minutes and hours, days, weeks, months and years.

"My Peace I Give"

THIS WAS THE night of Gethsemane, and there were many things the Son of Man had to say to His disciples. He spoke to them of love and of brotherhood, of light and of faith, of truth and of life; and now He was saying:

"Peace I leave with you, my peace I give unto you: not as the world giveth, give I unto you. Let not your heart be troubled, neither let it be afraid."

It was appropriate that on this night of treachery the word *peace* should be on His lips. It was a word that was heard in the angels' song on the morning of His birth. It was a Gift the disciples were asked to share when He sent them out to heal the sick:

"And when ye come into an house, salute it.

"And if the house be worthy, let your peace come upon it; but if it be not worthy, let your peace return to you."

Deep was the peace He gave. He asked only that those who received know that what was given, was given not for them to protect, but given that *they* might be protected.

The Son of Man knew there is no peace apart from God; that truth, brotherhood, faith, light, and love are its allies —and where this peace is, there is no evil.

Pontius Pilate

THERE WAS a night of questioning and, in the light of two candles placed so, from their places of concealment behind a partition, witnesses might testify they "saw him," the same witnesses were summoned to say what pieces of silver had paid them to say.

With the approach of morning the decision was made. Now the high priest was in need of an excuse. He could impose the penalty of death, but only the Roman governor could enforce it.

And so, "when the morning was come ... and they had

bound him, they led *him* away, and delivered him to Pontius Pilate."

Lest they should be defiled and not able to take of the passover, the high priest and the members of the Sanhedrin did not enter the judgment hall. Instead, they sent word, and Pilate came out to inquire: "What accusation bring ye against this man?"

Unctuously, they answered: "If he were not a malefactor we would not have delivered him up unto thee."

Impatient with them, Pilate cried: "Take ye him, and judge him according to thy law."

They refused, reminding Pilate: "It is not lawful for us to put any man to death."

Returning to the judgment hall, Pilate questioned Jesus, went back, and told the priests, "I find no fault in this man."

Again the words of the Roman governor were rejected. A second time Pilate questioned the Accused. Again he went out; and this time Jesus was with him as Pilate sought to persuade the chief priests: "Behold, I bring him forth to you, that ye may know that I find no fault in him."

As one voice, they shouted: "Crucify *him,* crucify *him.*"

"Take ye him, and crucify *him,*" shouted back Pilate, "for I find no fault in him."

Angry voices clamored: "We have a law, and by our law he ought to die, because he made himself the Son of God."

Motioning Jesus to come with him, Pilate went into the judgment hall a third time, inquiring as he did so: "Whence art thou?"

Waiting for an answer, and receiving none, Pilate cautioned: "Speakest thou not unto me? Knowest thou not that I have power to crucify thee, and have power to release thee?"

"Thou couldest have no power *at all* against me," answered Jesus, "except it were given thee from above: therefore he that delivered me unto thee hath the greater sin."

A fourth time Pilate tried to free the Accused—and now it was that the high priest tricked the Roman governor. In need of an excuse for the enforcement of the death penalty, and sanctimoniously using loyalty to Caesar as that excuse, the high priest warned: "If thou let this man go, thou art not Caesar's friend: whosoever maketh himself a king speaketh against Caesar."

Fearful of the political influence of the Sanhedrin, Pilate "brought Jesus forth, and sat down in the judgment seat in a place that is called the Pavement, but in the Hebrew, Gabbatha.

"And it was the preparation of the passover, and about

the sixth hour: and he saith unto the Jews, Behold your King! But they cried out, Away with *him,* away with *him,* crucify him. Pilate saith unto them, Shall I crucify your King? The chief priests answered, We have no king but Caesar.

"Then delivered he him therefore unto them to be crucified. And they took Jesus, and led *him* away."

ॐॐॐ

To the end of his days, Pilate must have remembered the One who stood before him in the judgment hall:

"Thou sayest that I am a king. To this end was I born, and for this cause came I into the world, that I should bear witness unto the truth. Everyone that is of the truth heareth my voice...."

Over and over and over, Pontius Pilate must have asked himself, "Who was this Man who, with death so near, could free me of blame, and free His accusers of blame, by saying:

" 'To this end was I born, for this cause came I into the world, that I should bear witness unto the truth.' "

On This Judgment Day

JUDAS ISCARIOT was alone with his thirty pieces of silver; Peter was at the door of the palace of the high priest, denying he was one of Jesus' disciples; Jesus was a prisoner in the palace.

When morning came, bringing the judgment of Pilate, Judas Iscariot went to the temple and sought out the chief priests, saying: "I have betrayed the innocent blood."

"What *is that* to us?" they scoffed.

Throwing from him the thirty pieces of silver they had given him to betray the Son of Man, Judas Iscariot left the temple, his eyes avoiding the eyes of other men.

At last he knew that when Jesus had spoken of "the kingdom of God," He meant the Kingdom of Spirit.

The words "kingdom of God" were not strange to Judas Iscariot when he became one of the twelve disciples; nor were they strange words in the town of Kerioth where, as the son of Simon, he first heard of Jesus. Often the prophets had used the words, but never in the moral sense that Jesus applied them.

It had taken Judas Iscariot almost three years to comprehend that the One who chose serving God to having authority over "all the kingdoms of the world, and the glory of them," could not be tempted to do as the son of Simon had thought—set up a kingdom wherein He, Jesus, was king; and he, Judas Iscariot, was a prince.

On this judgment day the son of Simon perceived that the One in whose voice was authority, even over death, was speaking of the kingdom in which all men are brothers—and finally understood the words:

"The hireling fleeth, because he is an hireling, and careth not for the sheep. I am the good shepherd, and know my *sheep,* and am known of mine. As the Father knoweth me, even so know I the Father: and I lay down my life for the sheep. And other sheep I have, which are not of this fold: them also I must bring, and they shall hear my voice; and there shall be one fold, *and* one shepherd."

Remorse tearing at his heart, the son of Simon "went and hanged himself. And the chief priests took the silver pieces, and said, It is not lawful for to put them in the treasury, because it is the price of blood. And they took counsel, and bought with them the potter's field, to bury strangers in."

Simon, the Countryman

DIMLY SEEN over the heads of the jeering, ecclesiastical mob, the Condemned, bent under the burden of carrying the instrument of His own execution, held the countryman's eyes as the escort of soldiers marched through the narrow streets of the still sleeping city, and toward a hill where the common thieves of Jerusalem were put to death.

The march passed close to the countryman, so close that the officer in charge of the soldiers ordered the countryman, who was from Cyrene and who was known as Simon, to carry the cross of the One whom the chief priests mocked as The King of the Jews.

Unshouldering the heavy burden on a hill called the place of the skull, or Golgotha, Simon, the Cyrenian, stood away as the executioners raised the three crosses—on one, The King of the Jews, and on each side, a thief.

After the executions were over, and Simon was again with his sons, Alexander and Rufus, he told them of the part he had played in the fulfillment of prophecy.

Soon, Simon was standing with his sons among the followers of the One whose cross he had carried—and treasuring the journey, and remembering the cross, not heavy now, but whose prints he would always feel across his shoulders, and on his back.

A Stone Was Sealed

THE CRUCIFIXION was over, but the chief priests still were uneasy on the next day. They remembered He had spoken of death, and had said, "After three days I will rise again"; and remembering, they went again to Pilate, this time to ask:

"Command therefore that the sepulchre be made sure until the third day, lest his disciples come by night, and steal him away, and say unto the people, He is risen from the dead."

Given their wish by the Roman governor, the chief priests "made the sepulchre sure, sealing the stone, and setting a watch."

It was after dawn on the third day that the two women, Mary Magdalene and Mary, the mother of James, came to the sepulchre, and found Him gone; and, later in that same morning, the soldiers went to the chief priests to report that, while they were on watch, the stone that sealed the sepulchre was rolled from the door, and the place where He had lain was empty.

So it was that, after reporting, the soldiers were offered money by the chief priests if they would say, "His disciples came by night and stole him *away* while we slept." They took the money, and said what they were paid to say. But what they said was lost in the testimony of His presence.

Mary Magdalene saw Him, and talked with Him, in the dawn of the day of Resurrection; Peter saw Him; two disciples walked with Him on the road to Emmaus; with Thomas absent, He appeared in the midst of ten disciples as they were gathered in an upper room in Jerusalem; eight days afterward, when Thomas was present, He appeared to His disciples a second time, saluting them with the traditional Jewish greeting, "Peace *be* unto you"; once He appeared to James; He appeared to Peter, Thomas, John and James and Nathaniel as they fished in the Sea of Galilee—and, before the Ascension, he met with His disciples on the Mount of Olives, and instructed them:

"All power is given unto me in heaven and in earth. Go

ye therefore, and teach all nations, baptizing them in the name of the Father, and of the Son, and of the Holy Ghost: Teaching them to observe all things whatsoever I have commanded you: and, lo, I am with you alway, *even* unto the end of the world."

Once, as Paul wrote about twenty-five years after the event, "he was seen of above five hundred brethren at once; of whom the greater part remain unto this present." *

Three times after the Ascension He appeared to Paul— once on the Damascus Road, once in Corinth, once when Paul was in prison in Jerusalem. After the Ascension, He appeared to John, on Patmos; and the author of the apocalypse set down His words:

"And the Spirit and the bride say, Come. And let him that heareth say, Come. And let him that is athirst come. And whosoever will, let him take the water of life freely."

Equally sublime were the words in the promise He made at the close of His visit:

"Lo, I am with you alway, *even* unto the end of the world."

* I Corinthians 15:6.

The Road to Emmaus

MANY TIMES He has come and has walked along the paths of men, as on the day when the two disciples were proceeding toward Emmaus talking of the Crucifixion, of the empty sepulchre and the linen clothes that had covered Him, and which had been put aside—of His words, "Destroy this temple, and in three days I will raise it up...."

As now, so then, flesh did not know Him, although He drew near and went with the two disciples, inquiring: "What manner of communications *are* these that ye have one to another, as ye walk, and are sad?"

Thinking Him a stranger in Jerusalem, they told of how three days before, "Jesus of Nazareth, which was a prophet mighty in deed and word before God and all the people," had been condemned to death, and was crucified.

All the way to Emmaus they talked of the execution. They told Him of the women who had gone to the sepulchre very early in the morning of this very day and who had "found not his body," but had "seen a vision of angels, which said that he was alive."

Doubting, they had done as the women had done, had seen what the women had seen, but had not seen Him.

Listening to the wonderment in their voices and in their words, the Stranger rebuked them: "O fools, and slow of heart to believe all that the prophets have spoken: Ought not Christ to have suffered these things, and to enter into his glory?"

And still they did not know Him, although walking with Him, and hearing His voice, and His words, albeit they had dwelt with Him in the land of Israel, with its ancient vineyards and their bitter grapes.

As they neared Emmaus, He saluted them in parting, but they insisted He remain with them.

And, "as he sat at meat with them, he took bread, and

blessed *it,* and brake, and gave to them. And their eyes were opened, and they knew him...."

❧❧❧

The question that tormented the two disciples throughout this day, and throughout the day before, and on the day of the Crucifixion, was answered.

Each Is Proof of the Other

JESUS WAS not of the synagogue, nor of the temple, as were the scribes, and the Pharisees, and the chief priests; but He preached in the synagogue and in the temple, and He knew the Law better than did they.

For the scribes, and the Pharisees, and the chief priests, tradition and ritual were the vessels of the Law; for Jesus, tradition and ritual were empty receptacles, and confirmation was in the heart.

For the scribes, and the Pharisees, and the chief priests, Jehovah was the historical God of *one* people; for Jesus, the Spirit of truth is the infinite God of *all* people—needing, not candles, but understanding to find.

And because He spoke as He did, they sought to trap Him in His own words, that they might turn the people from Him and "deliver him unto the power and authority of the governor."

᭒᭒᭒

There was the day in the temple when, listening as He taught the people, the chief priests approached Him:

"Master, we knowest that thou sayest and teachest rightly, neither acceptest thou the person *of any,* but teachest the way of God, truly," and asked:

"Is it lawful for us to give tribute unto Caesar, or no?"

Perceiving their deceit, Jesus inquired as to whose image was on a penny; and when they said, "Caesar's," he instructed them: "Render therefore unto Caesar the things which be Caesar's, and unto God the things which be God's.

"And they could not take hold of his words before the people: and they marvelled at his answer, and held their peace."

᭒᭒᭒

But at last, and in the early hours of the long night, they did trap Him, not before the people, but before themselves; for it was in the house of the high priest that they asked: "Art thou the Christ, the Son of the Blessed?"

When Jesus said, "I am," they questioned no further,

and agreed among themselves: "What need we any further witnesses? Ye have heard the blasphemy: what think ye?"

Nor were the people present when they brought Him before Pilate; nor when, at dawn, He was marched through the dim streets to the hill of execution.

They killed Him that the people might no longer hear His words, or see His works—for His words and His works could not be separated.

They remain indivisible, each as proof of the other.

The Search Is Within

Forty days had passed since the morning when, while it was yet dark, Mary Magdalene found the empty sepulchre. In the forty days, Jesus was seen many times, in many places, by many people. Now, while He talked with the eleven disciples on a summit near Bethany, He disappeared from their sight; and, as they sought Him, two strangers stood among them, saying:

"Ye men of Galilee, why stand ye gazing up into heaven? this same Jesus, which is taken up from you into heaven, shall so come in like manner as ye have seen him go into heaven."

In the years He was with them in the flesh, Jesus prepared His disciples for this day of His departure. They
were with Him in Jerusalem when Nicodemus, the Pharisee, came by night seeking word of the Kingdom of God;
and they heard Jesus say:

"Except a man be born again, he cannot see the kingdom of God."

Greatly perplexed, Nicodemus asked: "How can a man
be born when he is old?"

Answering, Jesus said that except as a man is "born of
water and *of* the Spirit, he cannot enter into the kingdom
of God"; explained, "That which is born of the flesh is
flesh; and that which is born of the Spirit is spirit"; and
counseled:

"Marvel not that I said unto thee, Ye must be born
again. The wind bloweth where it listeth, and thou hearest
the sound thereof, but canst not tell whence it cometh, and
whither it goeth: so is every one that is born of the
Spirit."

Accustomed to material proof and ancient argument,
the Pharisee did not perceive that Jesus was speaking not
of man born of woman, but of man created *in the image
of God*. Nor did the woman of Samaria perceive that Jesus

was calling upon her to be born again when, at the well of Jacob, He said to her:

"If thou knewest the gift of God, and who it is that saith to thee, Give me to drink; thou wouldest have asked of him, and he would have given thee living water."

She heard, but did not understand, his words, and the words He added: "God *is* a Spirit: and they that worship him must worship *him* in spirit and in truth."

The disciples wondered why Jesus talked thus with the woman of Samaria, but on the night of betrayal He chose for them the same subject He chose for her:

"Yet a little while, and the world seeth me no more; but ye see me: because I live, ye shall live also. At that day ye shall know that I *am* in my Father, and ye in me, and I in you. He that hath my commandments, and keepeth them, he it is that loveth me: and he that loveth me shall be loved of my Father, and I will love him, and will manifest myself to him."

One among them, Judas, not Iscariot, inquired:

"Lord, how is it that thou wilt manifest thyself to us, and not unto the world?"

And Jesus answered: "If a man love me, he will keep my words: and my Father will love him, and we will come unto him, and make our abode with him."

As it was on the day of the Ascension, when Jesus was lost to sight and the disciples searched for Him in a cloud, so it has been always; and so is it now.

The wind bloweth where it listeth, and thou hearest the sound thereof, but canst not tell whence it cometh, and whither it goeth: so is every one that is born of the Spirit.

Truly the Son of God, Jesus spoke often of the Kingdom; and said of it:

"The kingdom of God cometh not with observation. Neither shall they say, Lo here! or, lo there! for, behold, the kingdom of God is within you."

The Resurrection

SOME TWENTY YEARS after Mary Magdalene went to the sepulchre, Paul, the apostle, wrote:

"And that he was buried, and that he rose again on the third day according to the scriptures: And that he was seen of Cephas, then of the twelve: After that, he was seen of above five hundred brethren at once: of whom the greater part remain unto this present, but some are fallen asleep. After that, he was seen of James; then of all the apostles. And last of all he was seen of me also, as of one born out of due time."

Of this event, the event of the Resurrection, it may be

said it is a fact which invalidates the darkest superstition in the human mind—fear of death.

As such, it is the greatest fact in history.

It is the fact by which all facts are judged:

A Man walked the earth, and was not forsaken when crucified.

Apostle of the Gentiles

S AUL, THE PHARISEE, stood near and watched every stone
that was hurled against the kneeling Stephen; and
when the Christian was dead, the Pharisee seized men and
women from every Christian home in Jerusalem.

A Pharisee whose parents lived in Galilee before moving
to Tarsus, Saul hated Christians with a zeal that made his
name a symbol of persecution wherever Christianity was
taught. Taking his zeal to the chief priests in Jerusalem,
Saul asked that he be given letters to the synagogues in
Damascus that he might go there and bring back, for punishment, all who believed as did Stephen.

With the letters in his keeping, Saul was nearing Damascus when a great light swept over him. Blinded, he was taken by the hands of those who were with him, and led into Damascus.

Here he was sheltered not by those he came to greet, but those he came to seize. Ananias, a Christian, restored his sight; in the house of Judas, another Christian, he was fed that he might regain his strength. Soon, he was preaching in the synagogues, and declaring to the astonished congregations that the One he persecuted was, indeed, the Son of God.

Leaving Damascus where, by night, he escaped those who sought to kill him by being lowered over the wall in a basket, Saul, now known as Paul, preached in many places, as he had preached in Damascus.

Paul wrote many letters and built many churches, spoke of the Christ, preached of God, healed the sick, restored the dead, and called upon all mankind as he called upon the Romans, "Be ye transformed by the renewing of your mind, that ye may prove what *is* that good, and acceptable, and perfect, will of God."

Saul the Pharisee did not know what Paul the apostle came to know. Saul the Pharisee did not know that true growth is not in numbers, nor in countries occupied, nor in churches built—but in the vast, unexplored kingdom of the mind.

Nor would Saul the Pharisee have understood the words which, awaiting execution, Paul wrote to Timothy:

"For I am now ready to be offered, and the time of my departure is at hand.

"I have fought the good fight, I have finished *my* course, I have kept the faith.'

So Is No Man Common

MAKING INQUIRY for Peter at the home of Simon, a tanner, in Joppa, were three men. One was a soldier and two were servants of the household of Cornelius, a centurion in Caesarea.

Coming down from the housetop where he had gone to pray, Peter presented himself saying, "I am he whom ye seek: what *is* the cause wherefore ye are come?"

And they told him they had come because Cornelius "was warned from God by an holy angel to send for thee into his house, and to hear words of thee."

On the day following, Peter went with them to Caesarea,

where Cornelius met him, and fell at his feet in worship. Whereupon Peter lifted up the centurion, and rebuked him, saying, "Stand up; I myself also am a man." Going with the centurion to his house where others were gathered, Peter explained his presence among them:

"Ye know how that it is an unlawful thing for a man that is a Jew to keep company, or come unto one of another nation; but God hath shewed me that I should not call any man common or unclean."

❧❧❧

Daily, Peter walked with Jesus over the hills and over the plains of Palestine. He was with Jesus when He preached to the multitudes by the Sea of Galilee; he was with Him when He fed the five thousand; he saw the sick healed, and the dead restored; with James and John he witnessed the Transfiguration; was first among men to recognize Jesus as "the Christ, the Son of the living God"; sat with Him at the Last Supper; was with Him as He prayed in Gethsemane; saw Him, sat with Him, and ate with Him after the Crucifixion—and yet Peter did not perceive, as he came to perceive, that God "is no respecter of persons."

It was in Joppa, while the soldier and the servants of the

centurion were waiting at the gate, that Peter came to understand what he had not understood. He came to see that as all men are the children of God, so is no man insignificant, or common; nor can he be.

The Chalice

For almost fifty years Annas, his five sons, and Caiaphas, his son-in-law, ruled as high priests in Jerusalem.

Caiaphas was the high priest in the year of the Crucifixion. It was he who, after the restoration of Lazarus, called the chief priests and Pharisees together, and said to them, "It is expedient for us, that one man should die... that the whole nation perish not."

And from that moment they counseled together to put Jesus to death.

They feared, and they greatly feared, this Man who chose to speak of God over augmentation concerning tradition, and the Law. They remembered that when He purged the temple, He said to them: "Destroy this temple, and in three days I will raise it up."

Annas and Caiaphas did not know that "he spake of the temple of the body"; but they did know that what affected their temple affected their wealth, and their authority. So it was that Jesus was brought to the home of Caiaphas after He was taken in the garden. First questioned by Annas, He was bound and set before Caiaphas that He might be delivered to Pilate.

And now Peter and John were before Annas and Caiaphas and the clergy of the temple. Peter had healed the man who was crippled from birth and, with John, had taught the people and preached of the Resurrection of Jesus.

Seeking doctrine for which to punish them, the high priest asked: "By what power, or by what name, have ye done this?"

Boldly, Peter answered:

"Be it known unto you all, and to all the people of Israel, that by the name of Jesus Christ of Nazareth, whom ye crucified, whom God raised from the dead, *even* by him doth this man stand here before you whole."

Fearing the people because the number that believed was about five thousand, which was a tenth of the population of Jerusalem, the high priest "commanded them not to speak at all nor teach in the name of Jesus," and let them go.

Disobeying the command, the disciples continued to preach and to heal the sick that were carried into the streets of Jerusalem, and the sick that were brought from the cities close by Jerusalem.

In a rage, the chief priest ordered their arrest and imprisonment; and they were put in the common prison.

Early in the following morning, the high priest and the chief priests gathered together in the temple to sit in judgment upon the apostles when word came that, even now, having been freed by "the angel of the Lord," Peter and John were preaching in the temple.

Disbelieving, the high priest and the chief priests heard the officers say:

"The prison truly we found shut with all safety, and the keepers standing without before the doors: but when we had opened, we found no man within."

Nor did the high priest and the chief priests believe until they heard from one who came to them saying: "Behold, the men whom ye put in prison are standing in the temple, and teaching the people."

Still fearing the people, the high priest sent the captain of the temple with the officers to where Peter and John were, and instructed them to bring the apostles before the council, but to do so without violence lest they be stoned.

This the captain and the officers did, and when they were delivered, Peter and John heard the voice of Caiaphas:

"Did we not straitly command you that ye should not teach in this name? and, behold, ye have filled Jerusalem with your doctrine, and intend to bring this man's blood upon us."

Answering, the apostles said: "We ought to obey God rather than men"; and declared: "The God of our fathers raised up Jesus, whom ye slew and hanged on a tree; Him hath God exalted with his right hand *to be* a Prince and a Saviour, for to give repentance to Israel, and forgiveness of sins.

"And we are his witnesses of these things; and *so is* also the Holy Ghost, whom God hath given to them that obey him."

Having heard these words, the high priest and the chief priests agreed among themselves to kill them.

There was one among them a Pharisee named Gamaliel, a doctor of the law, who was not influenced by fear, nor persuaded by numbers. Standing forth, Gamaliel said:

"Ye men of Israel, take heed to yourselves what ye intend to do as touching these men," and urged:

"Refrain from these men, and let them alone: for if this counsel or this work be of men, it will come to nought:

"But if it be of God, ye cannot overthrow it; lest haply ye be found even to fight against God."

In the presence of the council, Annas, his five sons, and Caiaphas, his son-in-law, agreed with Gamaliel; but outside, it was Hanan, the son of Annas, who ordered the death, by stoning, of James, the brother of Jesus.

Annas, his five sons, and Caiaphas, his son-in-law, saw only the treasury and the power and never found, in the temple, the chalice the humble were always able to find.

Sunday

MORE THAN nineteen hundred years have passed since He walked along the shore of Gennesareth and saw Peter; since Pilate and Herod were friends together; since Peter, standing before Annas, the high priest, and before Caiaphas, reminded them of the day they chose Barabbas.

The thrones of Pilate and Herod are vacant and the seed of Annas and Caiaphas is scattered, but there is a day called Sunday when people put down their work in honor of the Christ of Easter.

This miracle called Sunday had its beginnings when a

few of His followers began gathering early on the first day of the week, before going to their work—to speak of Him, to recall things He had said, to remember places they had been with Him, to keep in mind the mission of His healings, to join in prayer and in singing a hymn, as He had done in the evening of Gethsemane.

So its beginnings—a few moments early in the day before people went to work and, finally, the day itself.

As the Jewish Sabbath finds its authenticity in the Ten Commandments, so with the Christian Sunday, although centuries before the trumpet was heard on Mount Sinai, the Akkadians, a pastoral people living in the lower Euphrates valley in 1700 B.C., were observing one day in seven, were calling the day Sabatu, and were speaking of it as "the day of rest for the heart."

Observance of the day called Sabatu and the religion of the Akkadians, with its sacrifices to the moon-god, and its worship of the planets, spread across Asia Minor.

It was ritual and sacrific that, still in flower a thousand and seven hundred years afterward, troubled the apostle Paul; and troubled him greatly. During his imprisonment in Rome (60-64 A.D.) Paul wrote in warning to his Christian converts in Colossae:

"Let no man therefore judge you in meat, or in drink, or in respect of an holyday, or of the new moon, or of the Sabbath *days.*"

Under guard in the time of his years in Rome, and executed, probably, by Nero during the slaughter of the Christians after the great fire in 64, Paul's work of organizing the Christian church did not die with him. Some two hundred and fifty years after Nero's savagery, another Roman emperor, Constantine, honored the One now heard by him, and first heard by Paul on the road to Damascus, by setting aside Sunday as a day of rest from "labour, excepting farming." The year was 321.

In 578, the Council of Auxerre decreed that "on the Lord's Day it is not permitted to yoke oxen or to perform any other work"; and, in 813, Charlemagne ordered the stopping of "all servile labor on the Lord's Day." Centuries have passed since Charlemagne was crowned emperor of the Holy Roman Empire, and in the more than ten centuries since Charlemagne there have been more than fifty thousand Sundays, all in remembrance of a Man who was hanged between two thieves.

❧❧❧

More than nineteen hundred years have passed since the Stranger called to Peter and his brother, Andrew; to James and his brother, John, "Follow me"; a hundred thousand Sundays have lighted their candles along the years since the moment of remembrance in the early morning of the first day of the week.

Now, wherever there are ears that hear the music of Sunday, hands are idle, and over the land is benediction. It takes one day in seven, does Sunday, or almost two months in each year—yet, with the taking, there is no loss; only gain.

Life Is Eternal

To LIVE forever is as natural as to live for a moment.
The miracle is not that life is eternal; the miracle is
that we live at all.

The awareness of being of life for a moment is the rev-
elation that we are of it forever.